THE WOMAN GOD USES

Favour.A.

All scripture quotations are from the King James versions and The Passion Translation versions, unless otherwise stated.

DEDICATION

I dedicate this book to God almighty the alpha and omega, my Father, to Jesus the author and finisher of my faith and to the Holy Spirit my guidance and my standby.

Also, to women out there who feel less confident of themselves or who want to develop a closer walk with God. To those who are yet to discover themselves in Abba and in the scriptures, to those who feel God is distant from them and are yet to discover his love and to those who feel they cannot be used by God, to those willing to make impact in their generation, this is for you.

CONTENTS

PREFACE

We are in the days when we don't have time to play religion. We are in the last days; the days of revival. These are the most crucial days when we need to be sensitive to the Holy Spirit's leading and allow God work through us. We are in the days when great achievements have no regard for gender because God is no respecter of persons.

Greatness is embedded in us; it is time to seek first the kingdom of God and be everything God wants us to be. As we surrender ourselves to God, our past failures and shortcomings won't be able to hold us down anymore.

The beautiful thing is God cares about us and he wants us to reflect his glory. God wants women who will remain loyal to Him; women who have left the affection stage of just confessing their love for Jesus but rather people who are truly devoted to him.

God gave us emotions and feelings; he gave us a will. He did that purposely so that he could communicate with us. He didn't make robots and he is never going to seize our will from us because he wants us to come to that point in our lives when we are fully yielded to him, not because he forced us to but because we have chosen to surrender to him.

When we come to the consciousness of God's will for us, we surrender gradually till we are filled with the fullness of God. This call is not for some special or specific group of women but for everybody regardless of your race, background, flaws and many more.

Chapter 1

The saved woman

Jesus answered, Nicodemus, listen to this eternal truth: Before a person can perceive God's kingdom realm, they must first experience a rebirth.

John 3: 3 (TPT)

Jesus was telling Nicodemus here; that if he desires to entire God's kingdom realm there is need for a rebirth. The woman who desires a relationship with the father, and desires to become a woman of impact has to be a saved woman; a woman who has experienced a rebirth and is made brand new in Christ.

Now if anyone is enfolded into Christ, he has become an entirely new creation. All that is related to the old order has vanished. Behold everything is fresh and made new.

2nd Cor 5:17 (TPT)

Being in Christ makes us brand new (Completely new). The same way there is a difference between a brand-new product and a fairly used one. No matter how beautifully packaged a fairly used product is the one which is brand new stands out. In Christ Jesus, we are like that brand new product. Once saved, we are completely free from faults and guilt. Jesus paid the price for our redemption on the cross with his precious blood.

But the precious blood of Christ who like a spotless, unblemished lamb was sacrificed for us.

1st peter 1:19 (TPT)

The precious, sinless blood of Christ was shed for us on the cross to save us.

I have swept away your sins like a cloud. I have scattered your offenses like the morning mist. Oh, return to me, for I have paid the price to set you free.

Isaiah 44:22 (NLT)

From the above scripture, Jesus is saying dear daughter, I have blotted out your transgressions, your faults, your scars just return if you have gone back to the world. You may have been too deep in sin or think you are damaged beyond redemption; you may be broken, hurt or weary. You may have done it all wrong, "come to me" says Jesus. There is no one Jesus cannot save; he came purposely to the earth to save the lost; so we can live restored to God and reconciled in the body of Christ. And he came to mend broken hearts because he feels your pain. Jesus does not condemn us. He saved RAHAB THE HARLOT and Rahab became part of the genealogy of Jesus. God used Rahab to save the land of Israel.

Hebrews 8: 12 (MSG) says:

They will get to know me by being kindly forgiven, with the slate of their sins forever wiped clean.

This means, God will forget your errors, sins and it will be like you were never in sin because with God your past does not matter. He will make you spotless, shining and glorious to behold.

Jesus Christ came to the earth to seek and save those who are lost, to heal that broken woman, to rewrite your story, to redeem you just like he did for Rahab.

Hebrews 10: 1- 18 described how they had to offer bulls and goats in the Old Testament for their sanctification. What power has goats, bulls to remove our sins? Christ paid an eternal sacrifice with his blood on the cross.

He wanted you free from the accuser and from the captivity of sin, from being a slave to the devil from the filthy garment. Zech 3: 3 says: Now Joshua was clothed with filthy garments, and stood before the angel. Anyone in sin is clothed with filthy garments and this hinders our access to the father. For God, though so loving is too Holy to behold iniquity.

So now the case is closed. There remains no accusing voice of condemnation against those who are joined in life – union with Jesus the Anointed one.

Romans 8:1 (TPT)

God the greatest judge declared you innocent in the court above all courts, He closed the case the devil opened against you and Jesus our mediator of the new covenant, the advocate stood with you in that court to defend you and you were declared not guilty (Romans 8: 33). That is **only** if you are saved, then that frees you from guilt and condemnation but anyone who is not saved is under the condemnation of the devil. We have an adversary, the devil but much more we have an advocate whose name is Jesus and he is constantly interceding for us and he will never leave his office of advocating for us because he has no successor.

For this is how much God loved the world He gave his one and only, unique son as a gift. So now everyone who believes in him will never perish but experience everlasting life.

John 3:16 (TPT)

All you need is to believe in the one who was sent. His name is Jesus, to redeem you from sin. In John 19: 30 (TPT) He declared: '*It is finished, my bride*!' He redeemed you from the curse gotten from the first man and woman (Adam & Eve) right there on the cross. If you are not yet saved, Jesus wants you to open the door of your heart to him.

I had an encounter many years ago with this scripture, Rev 3:20 and right there I surrendered my life to Christ. Prior to that day, I used to see Christianity as a ritual. I often separated myself to pray because I grew up in a Christian home but I had no full understanding of relationship with the Father. However, that day I heard him say to me, "open your heart to me and let me be your lord". You see, God made you; He knows how the world works. Let him run your life and lead you in the path to follow (Isaiah 30:19). In him is peace, healing, fruitfulness, joy, rest, safety and many more. Come to Jesus today, and let him be your hide-out from all troubles of life.

The heart that believes in him receives the gift of the righteousness of God and then the mouth gives thanks to salvation.

Romans 10:10 (TPT)

All you need do is believe. If you want Jesus into your life today say this word of prayer:

Lord Jesus, I believe that you died for me on the cross, and paid the price for my redemption. Right now, I receive you into my life to be my lord and personal savior to deliver me from the snare of the devil, from my guilt, faults and scars. I open my heart to you lord Jesus come in today, come in to stay. I thank you Lord Jesus for saving me I am now part of the family of God. Help me to serve you till the very end in Jesus name I pray Amen.

Congratulations! You are saved and now part of the family of God. You are now declared righteous by God.

Zech 3: 4 says: ***And he answered and spake unto those that stood before him, saying, take away the filthy garments from him. And unto him he said, behold, I have caused thine iniquity to pass from thee, and I will clothe thee with change of raiment.*** Oh! What joy Christ has removed the filthy garment and clothed you with a change of garment; the garment of redemption, garment of joy in place of heaviness, garment of glory in place of shame.

And since they have ignored the righteousness God gives, wanting to be acceptable to God because of their own works, they have refused to submit to God's faith- righteousness. For Christ is the end of the law. And because of him, God has transferred his perfect righteousness to all who believe.

Romans 10: 3-4 (TPT)

You are already made righteous by God. Primarily, righteousness comes by faith in God. You now have eternal life according to Rom 6: 23 because your life is now joined in union with Jesus.

NEW LIFE IN CHRIST

Yet look at you now! Everything is new! Although you were once distant and far from God, now you have been brought delightfully close to him through the sacred blood of Jesus you have actually being united to Christ!
Our reconciling "peace" is Jesus! He has made Jew and non- Jew one in Christ. By dying as our sacrifice, he has broken down every wall of prejudice that separated us and has now made us equal through our union with Christ. Two have now become one, and we live restored to God and reconciled in the body of Christ. Through his crucifixion, hatred died.

And now, because we are united to Christ, we both have equal and direct access in the realm of the Holy spirit to come before the father!

So, you are not foreigners or guests, but rather you are the children of the city of the holy ones, with all the rights as families of the household of God.

Eph 2:13, 14, 16, 18, 19 (TPT)

Now that we are in Christ Jesus, our life has been made completely brand new. Everything is new! You are no longer the woman they used to know; no longer the woman with scars and faults; your past does not matter. You are brand new in Christ. Our new life in Christ, grants us direct access to the father. We are no more strangers; we are daughters of God. We are part of the family of God and we have access to all the rights as families of the household of God. God has broken every wall of prejudice that separated us and now there are no more barriers between us and God. We have God as our father, Jesus Christ as our brother, for he has been described the first born among the brethren. We are now sisters of Jesus. We have the Holy Spirit as our guide, helper, comforter, teacher and stand by. We are privileged people. Being in Christ gives us these great privileges. We have been created anew in Christ Jesus, so we can do the good things He planned for us long ago.

So now it's clear that a person is seen righteous in God's eye not by faith alone but by his works.

James 2: 24 (TPT)

Through our faith in Jesus, we became right with God. Primarily, righteousness comes by faith, in God, but righteousness is not completed without our works. For faith without works is dead. So if we were made righteous by God by our action of faith of believing in Jesus and confessing him as our Lord and savior, then it does not end there. Our faith in God will go beyond that point of rebirth and will grow into developing a closer walk with God. For at the point of salvation, we are babes in Christ. So now, there is a need to grow our walk with God. Just like babies grow physically, mentally and in all areas we are to grow and become matured women in Christ who can discern between what is genuinely good and what is not.

We will be looking in the next chapter on how to develop a closer walk with God which will enable us grow spiritually into godly women.

Chapter 2

Developing a closer walk with God

These grace ministries will function until we all attain oneness in the faith, until we all attain oneness in the faith, until we all experience the fullness of what it means to know the son of God, and finally we become one perfect man with the fully dimensions of spiritual maturity and fully developed in the abundance of Christ.

Eph 4: 13 (TPT)

We keep growing in Christ Jesus until we attain the stage of full dimensions of spiritual maturity where we are fully developed in the abundance of Christ.

Running the Race

As for us, we have all these great witnesses who encircle us like clouds. So we must let go of every wound that has pierced us and the sin we so easily fall into. Then we will be able to run life's marathon race with passion and determination, for the path has being already marked out before us.

Hebrews 12: 1 (TPT)

We are in a race because Christianity is a race and not a mere religion. The joy of it is that we are not alone. We have all of these great witnesses as described in Heb 12: 1. Just like Kenneth Hagin described in his book: Following God's Plan For Your Life, the saints in heaven are watching us and cheering us up as we keep running the Race. They are not concerned about the natural things of your life like when you eat, go to work, buy new clothes e.t.c. rather, they are interested in your spiritual life like getting saved, telling others about Jesus etc. They only see those spiritual events of your life.

In Heb 12: 1, Paul was saying let go of every wound that has pierced you, the hurt you have gone through, the person who has put you in pain;

and you just can't seem to let go. You need to let it go dear friend and every sin you so easily fall into be it jealousy, anger, gossiping, immorality of diverse kinds, so we can run the race set before us. They are weights that will hinder us from serving God purposefully and being the woman God uses.

Declaration: In the name of Jesus the Christ, I lay aside every weight, sin, hurt, unforgiveness by your grace dear lord help me to run freely the race set before me with passion and determination. Thank you, dear lord, for I am more than a conqueror in Jesus name amen.

The whole armor of God

Put on God's complete set of armor provided for us, so that you will be protected as you fight against the evil strategies of the accuser.

Put on truth as a belt to strengthen you to stand in triumph. Put on holiness as the protective armor that covers your heart.

Stand on your feet alert, and then you will be ready to share the blessings of peace.

In every battle, take faith as your wrap – around shield, for it is able to extinguish the blazing arrows coming at you from the evil one.

Embrace the power of salvation's full deliverance, like helmet to protect your thoughts from lies.

And take the mighty razor – sharp spirit word of the spoken word of God.

Eph 6: 11, 14- 17 (TPT)

The whole armor of God described here is likened to a man going on to the war front with his shield, helmet, belt, breast plate and sword for his defense. We need to constantly put on this whole armor of God to be able to fight against the evil strategies of the accuser. The devil is the accuser of brethren and without this armor of God we become defenseless, unable to quench the fiery darts of the devil. This whole armor of God is our identity as a soldier of Christ and because we are in constantly in a war with the devil, we need to be ever ready to fight.

Then an astonishing miracle- sign appeared in heaven. I saw a woman clothed with the brilliance of the sun, and the moon was under her feet. She was wearing on her head a victor's crown of twelve stars. Then the dragon became enraged and went off to make war against the remnant of her offspring who follow the commands of God and have the testimony of Jesus.

Rev 12:1,17(TPT)

And;

For though we live in the world, we do not wage war as the world does. The weapons we fight with are not the weapons of the world. On the contrary, they have divine power to demolish strongholds.

2 Cor 10: 3 – 4 (NIV)

Our spiritual weapons cannot be seen but are energized with divine power to dismantle the oppositions of the wicked. We capture like prisoners of war, every thought of sickness, death, low self-esteem, failure, defeat, poverty and every sinful thought and insist that it bow in obedience to Jesus. We are fully armed with this armor of God ready to conquer the devil for whatsoever is born of God overcometh the world and this is the victory that overcometh the world even our faith. 1 john 5:4

Declaration: I put on the whole armor of God, ready to dismantle all satanic strongholds and quench all the fiery darts of the devil. I belong to the Lord's army and I am an ambassador of Christ. Therefore, I put off everything in my life that does not represent Jesus; the ancient man and I put on the new man that depicts Jesus as a lifestyle. So help me lord, in Jesus name amen.

The Prayer Connection

Don't be pulled in a different direction or worried about a thing. Be saturated in prayer throughout each day, offering your faith – filled

requests before God with overflowing gratitude tell him every detail of your life.

Phil 4: 6 (TPT)

Prayer is communicating with your father. It is being in a relationship with God (Father to daughter relationship). Tell God your fears, doubts, worries, pain etc. That is what communicating with God means. Jesus taught the disciples a model of prayer in Luke 11: 2 - 4

I love what psalm 37: 4 - 6 says:

Make God the utmost delight and the pleasure of your life, and he will provide for you what you desire the most. Give God the right to direct your life, and as you trust him along the way you'll find he pulled it off perfectly! He will appear as your righteousness, as sure as the dawning of a new day. He will manifest as your justice, as sure and strong as the noonday sun.

Let God direct your life as you commit it to him in prayer. Quiet your heart in his presence and pray (Psalm 37:7). Jesus is the only one who can heal broken hearts. He can heal your body, your mind, your finances, your academics and your family. Jesus heals them all. Draw near to Jesus and carry your burden to him.

Are you weary, carrying a heavy burden? Then come to me. I will refreshen your life, for I am your oasis. Simply join your life with mine. Learn my ways and you will discover that I am easy to please. You will find refreshment and rest in me. For all that I require of you will be pleasant and easy to bear.

Matt 11: 28 – 30 (TPT)

There are times we worry, go through challenges, broken hearted, unable to let go of our past. Jesus is the way out of every of the hurdles we go through.

Let's look at some women in the bible who went through hard times and prayed to God and God saw them through:

Hannah. 1 Samuel 1: 10 – 11

Hannah prayed her heart out to God in prayer and God gave her the desire of her heart.

Esther. Esther 4: 15 – 16

When Esther was faced with this dilemma between putting herself in harm's way and remaining silent while those she loved were massacred, she committed herself to prayer and fasting and asked others to join her.

Interceding For Others

Be faithful to pray as intercessors who are fully alert and giving thanks to God.

Col 4: 2
(TPT)

We are called as believers to a life of intercession. In the book I read titled 'Becoming a prayer warrior', I learnt that prayer is a love response to the burden of others. Interceding for others is a sacrifice. Prayer starts with you and what you know to be the obvious facts as you bring them before God. Intercession begins and ends with God. It is bringing other people's needs to your prayer altar leaving your own needs aside. It is praying the heart of God. Interceding for others has to come from a heart of love. Matt 22: 37

It can be a prayer for a friend at school, your work place, neighbor who is not yet saved, someone in church who is sick or helpless, someone you know that is hurting, praying for a family member or church member who has backslidden to come back to Christ.

Praying this kind of prayer at first may not be easy but it is the sweetest prayer you can pray because praying from your heart for others makes you feel delighted than praying for your own needs.

Pray for all men with all forms of prayer and requests as you intercede with intense passion. And pray for every political leader and representative, so that we will live tranquil, undisturbed lives as we worship the awe – inspiring God with pure hearts.

It is pleasing to our savior to pray for them. He longs for everyone to embrace his life and return to the full knowledge of the truth.

1Timothy 2: 1 – 4

Prayer was the priority of Jesus here on earth (Luke 6: 12, Luke 5: 16, Mark 14: 23). Prayer is to be our priority because prayer is the way that we; his branches, draw nutrients from him; the vine (John 15: 5). So therefore, pray without ceasing 1 Thess 5: 17.

I love Miss Clara's prayer in WAR ROOM (a Christian movie)

Pray this revival prayer:

You've done it again, lord you've done it again.

You are good, and you are mighty, and you are merciful! And you keep taking care of me when I don't deserve it. Praise you Jesus, you are Lord….

Raise up more that will call upon your name.

Raise up those that love you, and seek you and trust you.

Raise them up lord! Raise them up!

Lord, we need a generation of believers who are not ashamed of the gospel!

We need an army of believers, Lord that hate to be lukewarm, and will stand on your word above all else!

I pray for unity among those that love you.

I pray you open their eyes so they can see your truth. I pray for your hand of protection and guidance.

Raise up a generation, Lord that will take light into this world: that will not compromise when under pressure: that will not cower, Lord, when others fall away.

Raise them up, Lord, that they will proclaim that there is salvation in the name of Jesus Christ!

Raise up warriors, Lord, who will fight on their knees, who will worship you with their whole hearts.

Lord, call us to battle, that we may proclaim king of kings, and Lord of Lords!

I pray these things with all my heart. Raise them up, Lord in Jesus name amen.

How do we pray?

- Begin your prayer with thanksgiving

On your feet now – applaud God! Bring a gift of laughter, sing yourselves into his presence. Know this: God is God, and God, God. He made us; we didn't make him. We are his people, his well tended sheep. Enter with the password: 'Thank you!' Make yourselves at home, talking praise. Thank him. Worship him.

Psalm 100: 1 – 4 (MSG)

Thanksgiving is the password to God's presence. Psalm 95: 1 – 3

Your prayer must begin and end with thanksgiving. Phil 4: 6 – 7.

- Pray in the name of Jesus. The name of Jesus is our access code to the Father.

Until now you have not been bold enough to ask the father for a single thing in my name, but now you can ask and keep on asking him!

And you can be sure that you will receive what you ask for, and your joy will have no limits

John 16: 24(TPT)

- Pray using the word of God. Isaiah 43: 26
- Pray in faith. Heb 11: 6 says: 'Let faith be the motivation behind your prayer'. See also; Luke 1: 45, Matt 11: 24. Whatever is not of faith is sin. Rom 14: 23
- Pray in the holy ghost.

And in a similar way, the Holy spirit takes hold of us in our human frailty to empower us in our weaknesses. For example, at times we don't even know how to pray, or know the best things to ask for. But the Holy spirit rises up within us to super – intercede on our behalf, pleading to God with emotional sighs too deep for words. God, the searcher of the heart, knows fully our longings, yet he also understands the desire of the spirit, because the Holy spirit passionately pleads before God for us, his Holy ones, in perfect harmony with God's plan and our destiny.

Rom 8: 26 – 27

Praying in the Holy Ghost helps us to pray according to the will of God. Praying in the Holy Ghost also helps us build up our Faith (Jude 1: 20).

Paul's prayer

Paul prayed a prayer for the church at Ephesus in the first and third chapter of the book of Ephesians. However, these prayers apply to us today as much as they did to the believers at Ephesus, because they were given by the Holy spirit.

My heart is always full and and overflowing with thanks to God for you as I constantly remember you in my prayers.

Ephesians 1: 16 (TPT)

Paul from verse 17 – 20 gives us an insight into Paul's prayers for them.

Pray this prayer: (Put your name there)

17 I pray that the Father of glory, the God of our lord Jesus Christ, would impart to ____ the riches of the spirit of wisdom and the spirit of revelation to know him through your deepening intimacy with him.

18 I pray that the light of God will illuminate the eyes of your imagination, flooding you with light, until you experience the full revelation of the hope of his calling that is, the wealth of God's glorious inheritance that he finds in us, his holy ones!

19 I pray that you will continually experience the immeasurable greatness of God's power made available to you through faith. Then your lives will be an advertisement of this immense power as it works through you! This is the mighty power.

Ephesians 1: 17 – 19 (TPT)

14 So I kneel humbly in awe before the father of our lord Jesus, the Messiah,

15 The perfect father of every father and child in heaven and on the earth.

16 And I pray that he would unveil within you the unlimited riches of his glory and favor until supernatural strength floods your innermost being with his divine might and explosive power.

17 Then, by constantly using your faith, the life of Christ will be released deep inside you, and the resting place of his love will become the very source and root of your life.

18-19 Then you will be very empowered to discover what every holy one experiences the great magnitude of the astonishing love of Christ in all its dimensions. How deeply intimate and far – fetching is his love! How enduring and inclusive it is! Endless love beyond measurement that transcends human understanding this extravagant love pours into you until you are filled to overflowing with the fullness of God!

20 Never doubt God's mighty power to work in you and accomplish all this. He will achieve infinitely more than your greatest request, your most unbelievable dream, and exceed your wildest imagination! He will outdo them all, for his miraculous power constantly energizes you.

Eph 3: 14 – 20 (TPT)

These were Paul's prayer for the church at Ephesus which applies to us too. Whenever I pray this prayer, I put my name there and personalize the prayers by saying 'me' wherever Paul said 'you'. As I prayed these prayers I received more light from the word, my faith in God grew more (Eph 3: 20). God's love for me became more real to me, I became more conscious of his extravagant love for me (Eph 3: 17 – 19). I advanced more spiritually and felt more intimate with the Father than I ever felt before.

Growing in the word

In the same way that nursing infants cry for milk, you must intensely crave the pure spiritual milk of God's word. For this milk will cause you to grow into maturity, fully nourished and strong for life.

1 peter 2:2 (TPT)

Milk is necessary for a baby to help fuel the baby's rapid growth and development so also, we need the word of God to grow.

What is in the word?

1) Sanctification.

How can a young person live a clean life? By carefully reading the map of your word.

Psalm 119:9 (MSG)

The word of God is a spiritual map that guides our affairs in life and tells us how to live. That is why David said in psalm 119:4 (TPT). God has prescribed the right way to live: Obeying his laws with all our hearts.

Sanctify them through thy truth: thy word is truth.

John 17: 7 (KJV)

2) Power over sin

You are only truly happy when you walk in total integrity, walking in the light of God's word.

What joy overwhelms everyone who keeps the way of God, those who seek him as their heart's passion! They will never do what's wrong but will always choose the paths of the Lord.

A person given to God's word but meditating and walking in it will do no iniquity because the word of God always put us in check.

Psalm 119: 1 – 3 (TPT)

Thy word have I hid in mine heart, that I might not sin against thee.

Psalm 119: 11

That is why David said in Prov 4: 23: "Keep thy heart with all diligence; for out of it are the issues of life."

3) Peace

Great peace, have they which love thy law: and nothing shall offend them.

Psalm 119: 165 (KJV)

The word of God gives peace from the troubles and cares of this world. Luke 10: 38- 42

4) Direction

Thy word is a lamp unto my feet, and a light unto my path.

Psalm 119: 105 (KJV)

The word of God gives divine direction. There is a need for us to desire spiritual growth. In Heb 5: 11 – 14, Paul was talking to the church the need to move on to full maturity and not get too comfortable with taking milk which is the stage of childhood.

For every spiritual infant who lives on milk is not yet pierced by the revelation of righteousness.

Heb 5: 13

The same way babies grow past milk as they grow and become more matured is the same way we as believers are to grow from milk to strong meat, to become women whose spiritual senses perceive heavenly matters; who understand the difference between what is truly excellent and what is harmful.

Growing in the knowledge of the son of God unto a perfect man.

Eph 4: 13b

Until we gain knowledge of whom we are in Christ, our redemptive rights in Christ then we are getting beyond milk.

Every scripture has been written by the Holy Spirit, the breath of God. It will empower you by its instruction and correction, giving you the strength to take the right direction and lead you deeper into the path of Godliness. Then you will be God's servant, fully mature and perfectly prepared to fulfill any assignment God gives you.

2 Timothy 3: 16 – 17 (TPT)

The word of God is the mind of God. The word of God instructs us and corrects us it tells us the right path to follow. The word of God gives divine direction. It gives you instructions on how to live as a woman in Christ. It helps you become the godly woman. It is in the word of God you can differentiate beneficial way of living from the harmful way. Constantly studying the word of God gives us the strength to stand out from the norms of the world and live a life pleasing to God. It takes us deeper into the path of godliness.

How do we grow in the word of God?

Receive the help of the Holy Spirit during your study of the word. Pray for revelation as you look into the word of God. When you pray before looking at the word of God, you see beyond the letters and gain access to the light in the word of God.

For the letter killeth but the spirit giveth life.

2Cor 3: 6

Light surges from the word. The Holy Spirit is the revealer of the truth. He speaks the mind of the father. When you look at the word of God with the help of the Holy Spirit, the eyes of your understanding become enlightened. You gain access to Rhema. Sometimes, the Holy Spirit will lead you to a scripture in the bible, sometimes you hear that still small voice and sometimes you hear his audible voice. Sometimes you just get revelation from the word in which you get a better understanding of the word of God.

If you have not received the Holy Spirit, you can go boldly to the throne of God to demand from it from the Father. It is your right in God to receive the gift of the Holy Spirit. You cannot get light from the word without the Holy Spirit. Without the help of the Holy Spirit the bible will become tiring when you are studying it, because there is no revelation, you end up interpreting the scriptures with your own understanding.

If imperfect parents know how to lovingly take care of their children and give them what they need, how much more will the perfect heavenly Father give the Holy Spirit's fullness when his children ask him.

Luke 11: 13 (TPT)

When you ask the father, he will give you the gift of the Holy Spirit.

Many years ago, after I got saved and got baptized in water, I was yet to receive the gift of the Holy Spirit. I went on a 4 days bible study with a genuine crave and thirst to receive the gift of the Holy Spirit and on the last day as I began to worship God, I received the Holy Spirit.

If you are yet to receive the gift of the Holy Spirit you can pray this prayer:

Dear heavenly father, I ask today in faith for the baptism of the Holy Spirit upon my life. I receive a release of the spirit of God upon my life right now because you said in your word that you will give the Holy Spirit to us when we ask of you. So, I stand on your word today, and I acknowledge Jesus as the baptizer and in the name of Jesus I receive the gift of the Holy Spirit. I welcome you Holy Spirit into my life, come and dwell in me. Thank you, Jesus in Jesus name, I prayed amen.

Therefore, to have an effective study life it is important we pray before looking at the word of God. Seek a quiet environment with an open heart ready to receive from him. Praying in the Holy Ghost tunes us to the frequency of Heaven. When we pray in the Holy Ghost, we build up ourselves up spiritually and also our spirit man becomes more alert to hear from him. Praying in the Holy Ghost is tuning in to the radio of heaven to get the news for the day. Journaling down what we read from the word of God, the revelations we have received.

In as much as studying the word of God on our own is important. We should not neglect the ministry of teaching priests. The book of Hebrews says we should be followers of those who through faith and patience received the promise.

And I will give you pastors according to mine heart, which shall feed you with knowledge and understanding.

Jer 3: 15 (KJV)

God has put in place ministers, pastors, teachers who will feed us with knowledge and understanding of God's word. God sent Moses as a prophet to the Israelites and the scripture says He made known his ways unto Moses and his acts to the children of Israel. God reveals insights to his prophets that you would not see because he has ordained them to feed us with the truths of God's word. There are some things you may not fully understand by looking at the word of God yourself but through the ministry of these teaching priests, God speaks to us and reveals his plan for our lives.

They are our today heroes of faith. Though still running the race, but have attained heights in their walk with God.

You are rising like the perfectly fitted stones of the temple; and your lives are being built up together upon the ideal foundation laid by the apostles and prophets, and best of all, you are connected to the Head cornerstone of the building, the Anointed one, Jesus Christ himself!

Luke 11: 13 (TPT)

Don't just listen to the word of truth and not respond to it, for that is the essence of self- deception. So always let his word become like poetry written and fulfilled by life! If you listen to the word and don't live out the message you hear, you become like the person who looks in the mirror of the word to discover the reflection of his face in the beginning. You perceive how God sees you in the mirror of the word, but then you go out and forget your divine origin. But those who set their gaze deeply into the perfecting law of liberty are fascinated by and respond to the truth they hear and are strengthened by it they experience God's blessing in all that they do!

James 1: 22 – 25 (TPT)

The bible is a mirror that shows us how God sees us. It reflects the mind of God concerning us.

Another very important way by which we can gain from the word of God is through responding to the truth we hear because this way we become strengthened and experience God's blessing. When we observe and do what we read and hear from the word of God we become more like him.

To get more acquainted with the word of God you can use a devotional, and also anointed books. I make use of women bible app which has devotionals and scriptures for the day and devotionals from Joyce Meyer ministries. I also read a lot of other anointed books. To get more understanding on how to grow in the word of God, read: Kenneth Hagin (Growing up spiritually).

Walking in Love

1 Cor 13: 1 – 13 describes the importance, characteristic of love.

You are always and dearly loved by God! So, robe yourself with virtues of God, since you have been divinely chosen to be holy. Be merciful as you endeavor to understand others, and be compassionate, showing kindness towards all. Be gentle and humble, unoffendable in your patience with others

Col 3: 12 (TPT)

Paul here describes the virtues of God which are embedded in love. I struggled with these for many years and yes still asking for grace to walk in true love; The love that doesn't take offence easily; the love that is gentle and kind towards all irrespective of wrong done; the love that doesn't stop loving. The God- kind of love, the love that is genuine, the love that doesn't get jealous at other people's blessings, and the love that doesn't boast of her achievements.

Even though I am still growing just like you friends, I always remind myself of Eph 4: 13: Till I grow in the knowledge of the son of God unto a perfect man.

For love is supreme and must flow through each of these virtues. Love becomes the mark of true maturity.

Col 3: 14

Here is how God's children can be clearly distinguished from the children of the evil one. Anyone who does not demonstrate righteousness and show love to fellow believers is not living with God as his source.

Yet we can be assured that we have been translated from spiritual death into spiritual life because we love the family of believers. A love less life remains spiritually dead.

If anyone sees a fellow believer in need and has the means to help him, yet he shows no pity and closes his heart against him, how is it even possible that God's love lives in him?

Beloved children, our love can't be an abstract theory we only talk about, but a way of life demonstrated through our loving deeds.

We know that the truth lives within us because we demonstrate love in action, which will reassure our hearts in his presence.

1 John 3: 10, 14, 17 – 19 (TPT)

This is one thing we have to be careful about living in love. Paul referred to a life void of love as spiritual death.

***Don't owe anything to anyone, except your outstanding debt to continually love one another, for the one who learns to love has fulfilled every requirement of the law. Love makes it impossible to harm others, so love fulfills all that the law requires*.**

Rom 13:8, 10 (TPT)

Love is a fulfillment of the law. In other words, if you are walking in love you are walking in God's will for your life, and it will be easy to follow his plan and purpose for you. Not only are we to walk in love towards others, but we are to love God. This means we are to put him first.

Love the lord your God with every passion of your heart, with all the energy of your being, and with every thought that is within you.

Matt 22: 37 (TPT)

One of the strongest proofs of our love to God is sacrifice. Sacrificing our time, energy, resources, everything. Love comes from a heart of genuine passion towards God.

And in John 14: 14 Jesus said 'Loving me empowers you to obey my commands.' It gets easier to obey God's commandments if we walk in love towards God. And we know that His commandments are not grievous.

How can we walk in love effectively? Through the help of the Holy Spirit.

And this hope is not a disappointing fantasy, because we can experience the endless love of God cascading into our hearts through the Holy Spirit who lives in us.

Romans 5:5 (TPT)

The Holy Spirit empowers us to walk in love for God. The Holy Spirit puts us in check; He is always there to correct us when we are in the wrong. The Holy Spirit is a gentle loving person (He is a spirit that has a personality). The Holy Spirit makes God real to us. John 14: 16 – 17. This is the beauty of it even when we go into sin, even when we are in the wrong; the Holy Spirit never leaves us for He never condemns us. Jesus our advocate is always there at the right side of the Father advocating for us.

So now every righteous requirement of the law can be fulfilled through the Anointed one living his life in us. And we are free to live, not according to the flesh, but by the dynamic power of the Holy Spirit!

Romans 8:4 (TPT)

Prayer: Father, in the name of Jesus by the empowerment of the Holy Spirit I receive the spirit of love upon my life afresh. Help me Lord Jesus to walk in genuine love for you and towards others around me. I receive grace Lord Jesus to let go anyone who has hurt me, help me lord to forgive. Right now, I receive grace. Thank you, Lord Jesus in Jesus name amen.

Fellowshipping with the saints

So now we must cling tightly to the hope that lives within us, knowing that God always keeps his promises!

Discover creative ways to encourage others and to motivate them towards acts of compassion, doing beautiful works as expression of love.

This is not the time to pull away and neglect meeting together, as some have formed the habit of doing, because we need each other! In fact, we should come together even more frequently, eager to encourage and urge each other onward as we anticipate the day dawning.

Heb 10: 23 – 25 (TPT)

Fellowship is a mutual bond that believers have with Christ that puts us in deep, eternal relationship with one another. Fellowshipping with one another helps us grow.

Every believer was faithfully devoted to following the teachings of the apostles. Their hearts were mutually linked to one another, sharing communion and coming together regularly for prayer. A deep sense of holy awe swept over everyone, and the apostles performed many miraculous signs and wonders. All the believers were in fellowship with one another, and they shared with one another whatever they had.

Acts 2: 42 – 46 (TPT)

Benefits of appearing at the presence of God and fellowshipping with the saints.

1. We experience unusual joy at the presence of God. Psalm 16: 11 says: thou will show me the path of life: in thy presence is fullness of joy; at thy right hand there are pleasures for evermore. Are you feeling cast down or weary? Then the presence of God is the place to go to. Whether during our personal fellowship with God, or fellowship with the saints, the presence of God is a joy bank. Sometimes our minds get clouded and even when we don't feel joy around us, the presence of God is where we experience joy because at his presence tears are wiped away and sorrow is turned to joy.
2. We enjoy unusual strength at the presence of God. Psalm 84: 7 says: '*They go from strength to strength, every one of them in Zion appeareth before the Lord.'*
3. The presence of God is a place of possessing our possession, a place of deliverance, a place of sanctification. Obadiah 1: 17 says: *'But upon mount Zion shall be deliverance, and there shall be holiness; and the house of Jacob shall possess her possessions.'* We draw closer to God when we go to his presence because we enjoy communion with him.

Chapter 3

Becoming a woman of impact

There are accounts of women used by God in the bible as change agents to their generation.

In Old Testaments, we have examples of women like Deborah, Esther etc. In New Testaments we have women who were part of the ministry of Jesus like Mary the mother of Jesus Mary Magdalene, Mary of Bethany, Priscilla etc. We can see that God used women in ministry. God can use any woman provided we surrender ourselves to him. It may not necessarily be in full time ministry. Be it in business, academics, politics, medical profession, engineering etc. God can make use of any woman in this revival times.

Let's take a look at some of these women who were used by God in the Old Testament.

Rahab

Rahab was a harlot but God used her to save her household and the land of Israel because she hid the messengers which Joshua sent to spy out Jericho.

It was recorded of Rahab in Heb 11: 31 (TPT)

By faith the harlot Rahab perished not with them that believed not, when she had received the spies with peace.

Rahab was referred to as a woman of Faith. She became part of the heroes of Faith.

And it was told that the king of Jericho, saying, Behold there came women in hither to night the children of Israel to search out the country.

And the king of Jericho said unto Rahab, saying, bring forth the men that are come to thee, which are entered into thine house: for they be come to search out all the country.

And the woman took the two men, and hid them, and said thus, there came men unto me, but I wist not whence they were:

And it came to pass about the time of shutting the gate, when it was dark, that the men went out: Whither the men went I wot not: pursue after them quickly; for ye shall overtake them.

But she had hid them up to the roof of the house, and hid them with the stalks of flax, which she had laid in order upon the roof.

Joshua 2: 2 – 7 (KJV)

Rahab hid the spies who were against the king's order but this act of faith made her stand out and when Joshua was sent to deliver Israel from Jericho, Rahab was used by God as a helper to them.

And she said unto the men, I know that the lord hath given you the land, and that your terror is fallen upon us, and that all the inhabitants of the land faint because of you.

For we have heard how the Lord dried up the water of the red sea for you, when ye came out of Egypt; and what ye did unto the two kings of the Amorites, that were on the other side of Jordan, Sihon and Og, whom ye utterly destroyed.

And as soon as we had these things, our hearts did melt, neither did there remain any more courage in any man, because of you: for the Lord your God, he is God in heaven above, and in earth beneath.

Joshua 2: 9 – 11 (KJV)

She had heard about the events of the red sea, how they defeated the king of Amorites: Og and Sihon. She acknowledged God's mightiness like in Exodus 15: 11. Rahab knew that God had more power than the gods of Jericho.

And the same is true of Rahab who was found righteous in God's eyes by her works, for she received the spies into her home and helped them escape from the city by another route.

For just as a human body without the spirit is a dead corpse, so faith without the expression of good works is dead!

James 2: 25 – 26 (TPT)

Rahab was found righteous in God's eye by her faith in God. Rahab proved her faith by her good deed. Rahab became part of the genealogy of Jesus in Matt 1: 1, 5. Despite her past, her deeds were a proof of her faith in God and her faith was imputed unto her for righteousness. So, despite our past or background, God can use us as a savior to our generation.

Esther

Esther was an orphan raised by her uncle, Mordecai. At the time Queen Vashti dishonored the King, Esther became her replacement and got married to king Ahasuerus because she found favour in his sight. Esther 1: 10 – 19

In Esther 3: 1 – 15, Haman plotted to destroy the Jews (Esther's household) but in Esther 4: 4 – 16, Esther prayed and fasted to destroy Haman's evil plan. After the fast, though against the law, Esther showed courage by visiting the king without being sent for.

And they told Mordecai Esther's words. Then Mordecai commanded to answer Esther, Think not with thyself that thou shalt escape in the king's house, more than all the jews. For if thou altogether holdest thy peace at this time, then shall there enlargement and deliverance and deliverance arise to the Jews from another place; but thou and thy father's house shall be destroyed: and who knowest whether thou art come to the kingdom for such a time as this? Then Esther bade them return mordecai this answer, Go gather all the Jews, that are present in shushan, and fast ye for me, and neither eat nor drink three days, night or day: I also and my maidens will fast likewise; and so will I go unto the king, which is not according to the law: and if I perish, I perish.

Esther 4: 12 – 16 (KJV)

God who knows the end from the beginning knew a time would come when the Jews would be at the verge of being destroyed. (Esther 3:

13) God sent Esther as a deliverer for her people. If Esther had done nothing, she would have missed her assignment. Esther's position as a queen was God-ordained. If Esther had not saved the Jews, she might have been removed from her position as a queen and may have perished with the rest of the Jews. Esther became a savior to her generation.

Esther was confident in her God; she sought the Lord and He delivered her. James 5: 16 (TPT) says: 'For tremendous power is released through the passionate, heartfelt prayer of a godly believer'. Esther though perplexed went seeking God on the altar of prayer and fasting and received boldness. The presence of the Lord went with her. Exodus 14:14

Esther's statement of 'If I perish, I perish' meant 2 things: A confident woman and a selfless woman. She cared for the Jews more than her position because she knew that God sets a man up and pulls another down and if God placed her there and wanted her there, and since God had a covenant with the Israelites, He would come to her rescue.

Deborah

Deborah was a prophetess and a judge. She was the wife of Lapidoth. She judged Israel at that time. Deborah was a woman who heard from God concerning Israel (She had a prophetic gift). Deborah was a woman with strong connection with God and God used her to deliver Israel from the hands of Jabin, king of canan.

And she went and called Barak, the son of Abinoam out of Kedeshnaphtali, and said unto him, Hath not the Lord God of Israel commanded, saying, Go and draw toward mount Tabor, and take with three ten thousand men of the children of Naphtali of the children of Zebulun? And I will draw unto thee the river of Kishon Sisera, the captain of Jabin's army, with his chariots and his multitude; and I will deliver him into thine hand. And Barak said unto her, if thou wilt go with me, then I will go: but if thou wilt no go with me, then I will not go. And she said, I will surely go with thee: notwithstanding the journey that thou takest shall not be for thine honour; for the Lord shall sell sisera into the hand of a woman. And Deborah arose, and went with Barak to kedesh.

Judges 4: 6 – 9 (KJV)

Deborah was God's mouth piece for Israel. Barak knew that the presence of the Lord was so strong upon Deborah that he said 'if thou wilt not go, then I will not go.' Deborah referred to herself as a 'Mother in Israel' in Judges 5: 7. She referred to herself not as a Judge which judged the whole nation of Israel because of her wise counsel and pure judgment nor as a prophetess who God revealed things to concerning Israel but as a Mother in Israel. Her role as a mother in Israel showed responsibility and selflessness.

Characteristics of Deborah

- Deborah was a leader. Judges 4: 9
- Deborah was a woman of fairness and wisdom. Judges 4: 4 – 5.
- Deborah believed in prompt obedience to God's word. Judges 4: 9, 14.
- Deborah was a worshipping warrior. Judges 5: 1 – 5, 9 – 12. She knew the importance of thanksgiving and worship as a weapon of war as described in Psalm 149: 1 – 9.

Jael

Jael was the wife of Heber, the kenite. Jael was also used by God to rescue Israel. The Lord delivered Sisera the captain of Jabin's hosts into the hands of a woman as prophesied by Deborah and that was Jael. In Judges 4: 18 – 22.

In Judges 5: 24 – 27: Jael was described as a blessed woman. A woman God used to defeat Sisera which led to the deliverance of Israel from Jabin the king of canan.

Prayer:

Father, in the name of Jesus, I release myself to be used by you as a change agent, a savior to my generation in Jesus name amen. Obadiah 1: 21

Some other women in the New Testament were part of the ministry of Jesus and some lived an exemplary lifestyle as an inspiration to other women:

- Mary the mother of Jesus. Luke 1: 26 – 45. The woman God used to bring forth Jesus the Son of God to the earth. She was the medium through which Jesus was born to the world to save mankind.
- Mary Magdalene; Luke 8: 2 – 3 described a woman named Mary Magdalene who was oppressed of the devil and Jesus had delivered her and she followed and believed in Jesus. John 20: 13 she referred to Jesus as her Lord.
- Susanna and Joanna. Luke 8: 3. These women along with Mary Magdalene and many other women supported Jesus' ministry from their own personal finances.
- Mary of Bethany. Luke 10: 38 – 42. Mary sat at the feet of Jesus to learn from him.
- Martha. Luke 10: 38 – 42. Martha was hospitable as she opened her home to Jesus. Martha was worried and troubled about many things.
- Dorcas. Acts 9: 36 – 41. Dorcas was a woman full of good deeds.
- Phebe. Romans 16: 1 – 2. Phebe was a servant of God at the church.
- Euodia and Syntyche. Phil 4: 2 – 3. These women labored diligently in spreading the revelation of the gospel and they assisted greatly in Apostle Paul's ministry.

There are many women that were used by God in history as agents of change. Let's take a look at some of them; as we look into their biographies:

Mother Teresa

She was born in 1910 in Skopje, the capital of the Republic of Macedonia. At age of 18, she joined a group of nuns in Ireland where she was given permission to travel to India. She began working as a teacher but was moved by the widespread of poverty which led her to form a group (Order) "The Missionaries of Charity". Her mission was to look after the abandoned, the poor and destitute. She often mentioned the saying of Jesus "Whatever you do to the least of my brethren, you do it to me". And mother Teresa saying goes: "Love cannot remain by itself; it has no meaning. Love has to be put into action, and that action is service." In 1952, she opened a home for those who were dying and had no one to help so they can die with dignity. In her later years, she was more active in western developed countries and she commented that even though the West was materially prosperous, they were spiritually poor. Her whole life was influenced by her faith and religion but she confessed that sometimes she didn't feel the presence of God.

Amy Wilson Carmichael

She was an Irish Christian missionary in India who was born in Ireland in the year 1867. In 1982 she volunteered to the China inland mission but was rejected on health grounds (she suffered from neuralgia) but that didn't stop her passion for souls. However, in 1893 she sailed for Japan as the first kowick missionary to join the church missionary society (CMS) work led by Barclay Buxton. In 1985, she went to India for her health but ended up doing missionary work in India. She commenced evangelism with a band of women guided by the CMS missionary Thomas walker, where she was responsible for rescuing many women as well as little India children who were given to temple gods as well as little Indian children and little girls exposed to prostitution by their parents or grandparents. It then became her mission to rescue and raise those children and so Dohnavur Fellowship came into being and was registered in 1927. She was known at Dohnavur as 'Amma' (Mother), she was the leader and many came to know her through her writing. Although in 1931 due to arthritis she could not be physically engaged, she continued to write and appointed leaders to take her place. The Dohnavur Fellowship still continues today.

Esther Ahn Kim (Ahn Ei Sook)

Esther Ahn Kim was born on June 24, in 1908. Few years after her birth the empire of Japan annexed Korea and brought their religion where Koreans were forced to worship at Shinto Shrines and forced to pray to Japanese gods, dead emperors and former war heroes, while those who refused were sent to prison. This invasion led to the division of Ei Sook's family. Her mother followed Christ while her father's family chose to follow idol worship. Ei sook saw the significant difference between the life of her father and that of her father's family. There was misery in idol worship but in her mother's case there was happiness and peace. Her mother also told her often: "As you can see, idols have no power at all. The Lord Jesus is the only one who can give true happiness and peace." This made her trust in Jesus as well.

She studied in Japan and eventually returned to teach music in a Christian school. The Japanese leaders then threatened to close the school and torture anyone who refused to bow down to a Japanese Sun goddess. Everyone except Ei Sook bowed, so she was arrested but miraculously escaped to go into hiding. While she was in hiding, she prepared for her arrest and imprisonment by studying many chapters of the scriptures and committing them to memory since she wouldn't have access to the bible in the prison, subjecting her body to harsh conditions by going days without food and water and sleeping on the hard cold floor.

The Lord led her to the city of Pyongyang after coming out of hiding where she met Elder Park with whom she publicly called the Japanese government to repent, withdraw from Korea, and examine which was the true religion; Shintoism or Christianity. They were arrested immediately after the confrontation. She lived in a Japanese prison from 1939 to 1945 in Pyongyang where she and other prisoners were subjected to torture, hunger, extreme cold and hatred from female jailers. All these while, Ei sook continued to cry to God from strength. Many of her fellow prisoners accepted and trusted Christ because of the love she showed them.

On August 1945, Japan surrendered and the prisoners were released. Ei Sook moved to United States where she met and married a pastor named Dong Myun Kim. She continued to serve God until her death in 1997. She wrote a book titled: "If I perish, I perish."

Harriet Tubman

Harriet Tubman's birth date is unknown but her birth is estimated to be between 1820 and 1822 in Dorchester County, Mary land. At the age of 5, Harriet was rented out to her neighbors. Harriet was strongly against slavery and its abuse and this was observed in Harriet's as early as the age of 12 when she intervened to stop her master from beating an enslaved man who tried to escape, she was hit in the head by a two-pound weight and suffered from severe headaches and narcolepsy all her life.

In 1863, Harriet became head of an espionage and scout network for the Union Army. She also served as a nurse, a union spy, and a women's suffrage supporter.

Harriet was instrumental to the freedom and escape of over 300 slaves by leading them through an underground rail road. When asked how she was able to do this, she said she often listened to the voice of the Lord for direction. In 1896, Harriet purchased land adjacent to her home and opened the Harriet Tubman Home for Aged and indigent coloured people.

Agnes Okoh

Agnes Amanye Okoh was born in May 1905 to Onumba Emordi, a farmer and Ntonefu, a trader. She hailed from Ndoni Local Government in Rivers State, Nigeria. Out of the thirteen children her mother gave birth to, she was the only surviving child. Though her parents were not Christians, she worshipped periodically with a nearby Roman Catholic Congregation.

Agnes was not allowed to go to any of the numerous mission schools in Igbo land (the Eastern part of Nigeria). This is due to the gender discrimination that was prevalent then which believed that women do not belong in schools but in the kitchen of their husband's house. The little girls were involved in carrying water, collecting fire woods, rubbing floors, and initiated into trades rather than getting formal education.

Upon the death of her parents, she left her town to live with some relatives at Asaba, a town close to her mother's home town. In 1924, she married James okoh, a Ghanaian immigrant sailor in Nigeria. They then had two children; a boy and a girl. In 1930 her husband died and she decided to stay unmarried. Her only daughter died in 1938 and it was very difficult for Agnes to overcome that grief. Due to this, she developed chronic migraine and sought healing from hospitals. The migraine defied western medicine as well as traditional medicine. In the year 1942, she was healed of the migraine by prayers in the name of Jesus. The prayers were made by a prophetess whom she met through her friend. Agnes then began to serve God faithfully and believed in the healing power of Jesus. As years went by, she recognized that she had the gift of prophecy since all of her prophetic utterances were said to have been fulfilled. She was advised by her mentor prophetess Ozomena to be patient and wait and prepare but not rush into ministry.

In 1943, while returning from the market where she was a textile trader, she claimed to have heard a voice saying ‘Matthew 10’ repeatedly. She looked around but couldn’t find anyone talking to her. She then sought for a friend who was semi- literate who then sought for a young man who read the entire chapter to them. In 1947, she began ministerial work and preached using Matthew 10, as it was her favourite scripture. She preached on the road, in market, in villages and many surrendered their lives to Christ through her, many also got healed of various illnesses.

Agnes’ ministry was planted in many towns and villages. She became a refugee along with many others at the outbreak of civil war in Nigeria in 1967, but nothing stopped her from preaching the gospel, encouraging others and healing the sick in the name of Jesus. She could quote many scriptures verbatim even though she was unlearned as it was though, God wrote the scriptures in her brain. Many found it hard to believe that God used a woman to do such things and spread rumors that she was using ‘dark powers.’ They tried to kill her but failed, she was also mocked for her way of worship; clapping of hands and shouting of ‘hallelujah.’

There is no doubt that Agnes Okoh was instrumental to the spread of the gospel in Nigeria especially during the civil war. She was described as; a mother, a leader, a philanthropist, a selfless and brave woman. Agnes went to be with the lord in 10th March, 1995.

These are many great women who are being used by God in different fields. Let’s take a look at some of them in ministry today: Pastor Mrs. Faith Oyedepo, Pastor Mrs. Folu Adeboye, Pastor Mrs. Funke Felix Adejumo, Pastor Mrs. Becky Enenche, Joyce Meyer, and Priscilla Shirer. The list of these great women of today is endless. That includes you and me either presently or in the making. Being a woman of impact is not limited to ministry. We are meant to shine as lights in our various fields.

There is no one that cannot be used by God; God can work through you. Many times, we feel that the only people being really used by God are those who preach on the altar with a large congregation. God has given everyone of us different, unique and special assignments.

God's marvelous grace imparts to each one of us varying gifts and ministries that are uniquely ours. So, if God has given you the grace-gift of prophecy, you must activate your gift by using the proportion of faith you have to prophesy. If your grace-gift is serving, then thrive in serving others well. If you have the grace-gift of teaching, then be actively teaching and training others. If you have the grace-gift of encouragement, then use it often to encourage others. If you have the grace-gift of giving to meet the needs of others, then may you prosper in your generosity without any fan-fare. If you have the gift of leadership, be passionate about your leadership. And if you have the gift of showing compassion, then flourish in your cheerful display of compassion.

Romans 12: 6-8 (TPT)

Apostle Paul was describing here that we have different ministries, God has placed a special ministry for everyone which is to serve him. Everybody has been called into ministry; ministry of intercession and reconciliation.
We have seen in history and in the bible women who were used by God and there was one peculiar thing about them which was service; service to God and service to meet the needs of others. Many times, we desire spiritual gifts; God working special miracles through us. We need to understand that the first perquisite to being used by God is a call to serve. Signs and wonders will naturally flow when we serve God (having a steady walk with him) and believing in him.

God wants to use you, but you need to have a heart for him. God is looking for intercessors, people who are passionate to see souls saved, people who are willing and ready to help the broken, discouraged and helpless people out there. We can make Jesus known using every opportunity we have to bring many to his light. Let's shine as lights wherever we are, even if we end up working backstage and not known or appreciated. God sees and rewards every single service we do.

In Kenneth Hagin's book 'Fulfilling God's Plan for Your Life', I saw a prayer there; Pray this prayer from your heart:

Lord, I present myself to you. May your will be done in my life. May I never forget that I have surrendered all I am to you.

I commit myself to be the one whom you can use – consecrated and separated unto your purposes. I'll pay the price by denying the flesh. If you call me in the nighttime, I'll get on my knees and pray. If I am never seen of men, and if I always work behind the scenes, still I will be faithful.

I lay aside all personal ambition. I'll be one who walks in the spirit and in your perfect will. In Jesus name, your will shall be wrought in my heart, in my life, and in my ministry.

The Confident Woman

Being confident at times is one of the hardest things to do. There is a difference between feeling confident and actually being confident. A lot of times many women suffer from lack of confidence due to their past, background, status etc.

Let's look at the secrets to being confident:

1) A confident woman knows that she is loved. She does not look down on herself. She is conscious of the fact that God loves her.

And He chose us to be his very own, joining us to himself even before He laid the foundation of the universe! Because of his great love, he ordained us, so that we would be seen as holy in his eyes with an unstained innocence. For it was always in his perfect plan to adopt us as his delightful children, through our union with Jesus, the anointed one, so that his tremendous love that cascades over us would glorify his grace for the same love he has for his Beloved one, Jesus, he has for us. And this unfolding plan brings him great pleasure!

Eph 1: 4 – 6 (TPT)

I was not conscious of God's love even as a believer and could not receive his love. I did not believe God cared about any little detail about me other than my walk with him.

I have never quit loving you, and never will. Expect love, love and much love.

Jeremiah 31: 3 (MSG)

God is saying to his beloved daughter I have not stopped loving you and won't stop now so be conscious of my love for you, receive it so you can have the power to love others and be confident knowing for a fact that he loves you and you are not alone.

2) A confident woman knows she is helped by God. A confident woman sees and acknowledges God as her helper. She knows that since God is with her, she has nothing to be afraid of. She may have fallen; she may have missed it in the past but with God's help she rises higher than she ever imagined and even when she is broken, she knows God is ever with her.

And the master, God, stays right there and helps me, so I'm not disgraced. Therefore, I set my face like flint, confident that I will never regret this.

Isaiah 50:7 (MSG)

Esther certainly knew that God was right there to help her so she confidently went to the king knowing she would not regret it. Daniel also knew that God was always with him and therefore will deliver him from the Lion's den. A confident woman does not look at her present situation for she knows that help is coming from God.

3) A confident woman refuses to live in fear. Declarations of Faith are the only acceptable attitude we can have towards fear. That does not mean we will never feel fear, but it does not mean that we will never feel fear, but it does mean we will not allow it to rule our decisions and actions. 2 Timothy 1:7 says for God has not given us the spirit of fear, but of power, love and sound mind.

Believe in me so that rivers of living water will burst out from within you, flowing from your innermost being, just like the scripture says!

John 7: 38 (TPT)

Isaiah 41: 10, 13 (MSG) says;

Don't panic. I'm with you. There's no need to fear for I'm your God. I'll give you strength. I'll help you. I'll hold you steady. Keep a firm grip on you. That's right. Because I, your God, have a firm grip on you and I'm not letting go. I'm telling you 'Don't panic. I'm right here to help you'.

God is saying to you daughter don't panic.

4) A confident woman takes action.

Looking back at the story of Esther in the bible, when Haman plotted to destroy the Jews, Esther could have sat back and wait for something to happen instead of making something happen but after she went to God in prayer and fasting, she received confidence and went to the king so she could save her people from destruction. Another example; David when his wives and children were being carried away by the Amalekites that he inquired of the lord what to do and God told him to pursue, overtake and recover all. 1 Samuel 30: 1 – 8.

A naturally shy person has to overcome timidity, anxiety and low confidence.

God Honors Faith

Then Jesus went thence, and departed into coasts of tyre and Sidon. And, behold, a woman of canan came out of the same coasts, and cried unto him, saying, 'Have mercy on me, O Lord, thou son of David; my daughter is grievously vexed with a devil.' But he answered her not a word. And his disciples came and besought him, saying; send her away; for she crieth after us. But he answered and said, I am not sent but unto the lost sheep of the house of Israel. Then came she and worshipped him, saying, Lord, help me. But he answered and said, it is not meet to take the children's bread, and cast it to dogs. And she said, truth Lord: yet the dogs eat of the crumbs which fall from their master's table. Then Jesus answered and said unto her, O woman, great is thy faith: be it unto thee as thy wilt. And her daughter was made whole from that very hour.

Matthew 15: 21 – 28 (KJV)

The Canaanite woman refused to give up even when Jesus ignored her, she was persistent. She knew her daughter was oppressed of the devil and she was tired of her situation. The word 'Dog' as referred to in Rev 22: 15 meant there was no place in heaven for dogs that could mean she was not saved or maybe because she was not an Israelite. Either way, her answer in verse 27 qualified her as a woman of faith. She knew she was entitled to something even if she was a dog. Whether she deserved it or did not she was not going to give up. She was a confident woman. How much more when we are saved and are children of God, we should have more confidence to approach God because God honors Faith. Even Jesus had to applaud that woman and acknowledged her as a woman of great faith.

Hebrews 4: 16 (NIV) says; "Let us then approach God's throne of grace with confidence, so that we may receive mercy and find grace to help us in time of need."

5) A confident woman avoids comparisons

One of the major causes of lack of confidence is comparison. I was greatly involved in that. Sometimes we compare our look, stature, achievements, spiritual growth, personality, talents, and intelligence. I did all of that. I believe the best way in getting out of comparison is believing that we are all unique and different whether light- skinned, dark, tall, short, slim, fat, introverted, extroverted, out spoken, quiet, etc. For personality, a person may be choleric that kind of person is a born leader it means that kind of person often gets leadership positions, that kind of person is naturally bold, outspoken etc. God created us uniquely in his own image and comparing ourselves to other women or people in general does not go well with God. Remember that being different is good, celebrate your uniqueness, discover God's purpose for you and walk in it.

Here is a quote by Theodore Roosevelt:

"Comparison is the thief of Joy"

"Don't compare yourselves to others. You have no idea what their journey is all about."

"A flower does not think of competing to the flower next to it. It just blooms."

Each of you must examine your own actions. Then you can be proud of your own accomplishments without comparing yourself to others. Assume your own responsibility.

Galatians 6: 4 – 5 (GW)

Beauty and Self Worth

I looked it up online what beauty meant and by definition; a beautiful woman is a woman who is passionate about life, shows compassion, pursues learning, refuses to give up, and believes she is worthy.

Beauty is not limited to a particular complexion or body type.

How to improve your self-image:

- Stop comparing. We have discussed this earlier. Just know that we cannot all be the same. Comparison makes one feel inferior. For example; you cannot compare a rose to a lily, they are both beautiful and they are different.
- Change your thoughts. Know that you are more than skin. You have so much embedded in you, you have a purpose to fulfill and you are unique. You are you and no one else can be you.
- Give yourself total acceptance. I admit it took me a lot of time to accept myself. You need to feel confident in your skin and regardless of your body type love yourself.

  Beauty is confident so she doesn't need to wear revealing or indecent dresses. Beauty does not need to follow the world's system or definition of beauty. When you look in the mirror and see your flaws encourage yourself with these scriptures and you can pray that God helps you see yourself the way he sees you because that really helped me.

Bible verses:

You are altogether beautiful, my darling; there is no flaw in you.

SOS 4:7 (NIV)

You formed my innermost being, shaping my delicate inside and my intricate outside, and wove them all together in my mother's womb. I thank you, God, for making me so mysteriously complex! Everything you do is marvelously breathtaking. It simply amazes me to think about it! How thoroughly you know me, Lord! You even formed every bone in my body when you created me in the secrets place, carefully, skillfully shaping me from nothing to something. You saw who you created me to be before I became me!

Psalm 139: 13 – 16a (TPT)

But you are God's chosen treasure, priests who are kings, a spiritual 'nation' set apart as God's devoted ones. He called you out of darkness to experience his marvelous light, and now he claims you as his very own. He did this so that you would broadcast his glorious wonders throughout the world.

1 peter 2:9(TPT)

For we are God's workmanship, created in Christ Jesus for good works, which God prepared beforehand, that we should walk in them.

Eph 2:

But the Lord said to Samuel, 'Do not look on his appearance or on the height of his stature, because I have rejected him. For the Lord sees not as man sees: man looks on the outward appearance, but the Lord looks on the earth.

1 Samuel 16:7 (NIV)

Knowing who we are in Christ changes our thoughts and the way we see ourselves. We begin to see a better version of ourselves and see ourselves as God sees us and this makes us confident knowing our physical appearance is not really all that matters provided, we dress decently and nicely (neat and beautiful) but also our inward appearance and the things God wants to do through us.

Prayer: Father, in the name of Jesus I receive the spirit of confidence, I cast out every spirit of fear and anxiety for you have not given me the spirit of fear but of power, love and sound mind. I choose to be confident because I know you are with me at all times. Help me dear Lord Jesus to see myself the way you see me, as the apple of your eyes and to live with the consciousness that I am loved by you thank you Lord in Jesus name amen.

FINDING REST IN JESUS

Listen to me. Never let anxiety enter your hearts. Never worry about any of your needs, such as food or clothing. For your life is infinitely more than just food or the clothing you wear. Take the care free birds as your example. Do you ever see them worry? They don't grow their own food or put it in a storehouse for later. Yet God takes care of everyone of them, feeding each of them from his love and goodness. Isn't your life more precious to God than a bird? Be carefree in the care of God! Does worry add anything to your life? Can it add one year or one day? So, if worrying adds nothing, but actually subtracts from your life, why would you worry about God's care for you? Think about the lilies. They grow and become beautiful, not because they work hard or strive to clothe themselves. Yet not even Solomon, wearing his kingly garments of splendor, could be compared to a field of lilies. If God can clothe the fields and meadows with grass and flowers, can't he clothe you as well, o struggling one with so many doubts? Don't let worry enter your life. Live above the anxious cares about your personal needs. People everywhere seem to worry about making a living, but your heavenly father knows your every need and will take care of you. Each and every day he will supply your needs as you seek his kingdom passionately, above all else.

So don't ever be afraid, dearest friends! Your loving father joyously gives you his kingdom realm with all its promises!

Luke 12: 22 – 32 (TPT)

Jesus sees your cares and worries so commit them to God dear friend and let Him help you through your troubles for he is your burden bearer. Do you feel God is silent? There are times we don't hear from God and feel like God doesn't care about us or feel we have wronged God so he chose to neglect us. As long as you are walking in obedience to God's instructions, he is right there ready to help you. Do you feel empty, then go to Jesus, let him give you rest. Do you feel God is distant from you? He is right beside you never leaving you. The Holy Spirit is right there with you. I call him my 'stand by'. I once felt this void like I did not have a relationship with God I wanted more. I felt empty. I felt like God wanted so much from me and I felt drained. God looked far-fetched to me. I envied those people who heard the audible voice of God because I rarely did and I did not feel like God cared a dime about me. I felt I was just probably one of the people God created on earth to meet up a specific population He had in mind and some days if I slept off when I wanted to pray or pray for fewer minutes, the guilt of condemnation will hit me right hard throughout the day until I went to God in prayer and cried so hard at his feet, I really needed him to help me I really wanted to feel him and that day I felt him embrace me. I felt love and much love again. I heard welcome. And the Holy spirit led me to the book of Ephesians and Colossians. I began to study that and I began to understand God's love for me the more. So, if you feel this way and you will go to him, you will find out that he is right there waiting for you and ready to embrace you and welcome you and the good news is you get a welcome package.

The Holy spirit also directed me to Matthew 11: 28 – 30. The passion translation specifically:

"Are you weary, carrying a heavy burden? Then come to me. I will refresh your life, for I am your oasis. Simply join your life with mine. Learn my ways and you'll discover that I'm gentle, humble, easy to please, you will find refreshment and rest in me. For all that I require of you will be pleasant and easy to bear."

I learnt a lot of things from that scripture and that was:

Firstly, I began to see Jesus as my oasis and anytime I needed refreshment in my spirit. I found communicating with Abba so lovely to do. I learnt the act of spending time with God even if am not praying. I will go to him, worship him, talk to him and from there most times I find myself praying in the Holy ghost. That made my prayer life easier and my relationship with Him developed.

Secondly, I discovered that God is actually easy to please and I can find rest in Him in the midst of storms.

Following God's ways; finding peace through that.

But the who always listens to me will live undisturbed in a heavenly peace. Free from fear, confident and courageous you will rest unafraid and sheltered from the storms of life.

Prov 1: 33 (TPT)

When you make God your priority and live in obedience to his commands, he becomes your defense and you will live in undisturbed in a heavenly peace being confident that if God is with you, who then can be against you.

He becomes your personal bodyguard as you follow his ways, protecting and guarding you as you choose what is right.

Prov 2:7 - 8 (TPT)

When I found this scripture, I was marveled and kept on staring at it for a long time. The scripture describes how much God is willing and ready to protect his people. The righteous are those who are committed to doing what pleases him, those who choose what is right. That is why 1 Peter 3: 13 (TPT) says: "***Why would anyone harm you if you're passionate and devoted to pleasing God?"***

We can find so much rest and solace in God when we are passionate and devoted to pleasing Him. Then He is committed to guarding us and protecting us and because of that we have nothing to fear.

The Lord is my best friend and my shepherd. I always have more than enough.

He offers a resting place for me in his luxurious love. His tracks take me to an oasis of peace, the quiet brook of bliss.

That's where he restores and revives and my life. He opens before me pathways to God's pleasure and leads me along in his footsteps of righteousness so that I can bring honor to His name. Lord, even when your path takes me through the valley of deepest darkness, fear will never conquer me, for you already have! You remain close to me and lead me through it all the way. Your authority is my strength and my peace. The comfort of your love takes away my fear. I'll never be lonely, for you are near.

You become my delicious feast even when my enemies dare to fight. You anoint me with the fragrance of your Holy spirit; you give me all I can drink of you until my heart overflows. So why would I fear the future? For your goodness and love pursue me all the days of my life. Then afterward, when my life is through, I'll return to your glorious presence to be forever with you!

Proverbs 23: 1 – 6 (TPT)

One other way we can rest fully in God is being aware of His love for us. When you constantly remind yourself of God's love for you, it takes away fear from you. The Lord is our shepherd who will always lead the sheep that no one can harm. God is nearer to us than we think.

Chapter 4

Gaining Momentum

Momentum is generally used to describe increasing forward motion.

According to the Longman dictionary, Momentum is the ability to keep increasing, developing, or being more successful.

To gain momentum means to gain increase, to receive an increment in motion, to move forward.

There are various things that slow one down in the race of life. There are also things that serve as hindrances to we maximizing our full potential and getting to the height God has reserved for us. But now it's time to gain momentum.

Let's look at 3 keys to gaining momentum:

Speak Life to Yourself

Words kill, words give life; they are either poison or fruit – you choose.

Prov 18: 21(MSG)

Our words can either kill or give life. Our words are seeds and everyone reaps from it either poison or good fruit. Speak life to yourself and learn to speak God's word. Stop saying, 'I'm depressed', 'I'm discouraged' 'I just don't have any confidence'. Declare into your day; this is the day the Lord has made I'll rejoice and be glad in it. Declare positive things into the day. Declare into your future. Declare into the life of your family. For your words contain power. Keep meditating on the word so you can see God's plan for your life for his plans for you are of good and not of evil to give you a fulfilled end. As you spend time with the word of God your mind gets renewed and you begin to speak life to yourself for out of the abundance of the heart the mouth speaketh.

In the natural, 'seeing is believing', but in the kingdom we believe and then we see. For the just shall live by faith. What you see is what you speak. God asked prophet Jeremiah, "what seest thou?" the question is what do you see? God told Abraham as far as your eyes can see will I give to you. When we see God's promises concerning us from the scripture, we can confidently speak it to our life. What has God said concerning your health, home, academics, career, business, ministry or finances from the scriptures? Have you seen excellence, sound health, rest, breakthrough, divine protection and all that God wants you to enjoy? Then speak it.

Association

On their release, Peter and John went back to their own people and reported all that the chief priests and elder had said to them.

Acts 4: 23 (NIV)

The ESV translation said peter and john went back to their friends. They had their own people, their tribe, their friends and these friends were believers. In verse 24 they raised their voices to pray not to cry, cast their heads down but to pray! They were of one mind. Amos 3:3 (MSG) says: "Do two people walk hand in hand if they are not going to the same place?"

Two people cannot walk side by side, so closely unless they are going to the same place. There is always agreement in friendship because you can always choose your company. Not everyone belongs to your tribe; you must choose carefully people who will help you grow. Iron sharpeneth iron. An iron may still sharpen a wood into a sharp-mouthed wood and of which that iron will not benefit anyway so even if you have a friend you want to help to grow spiritually because we cannot completely avoid them, we must pull them out of the fire; Jude 4: 21, but we must still have another company where we ourselves are growing from because it is easier to pull someone down than to pull another up.

Keep being compassionate to those who still have doubts, and snatch others out of the fire to save them. Be merciful over and over to them, but always couple your mercy with the fear of God. Be extremely careful to keep yourselves free from the pollutions of the flesh.

Jude 1: 22 – 23 (TPT)

No matter how sharp an iron is it still needs another iron to sharpen it overtime to improve its state. Jude 4: 23 says be extremely careful because you want a person saved does not mean you follow the person to a club house or a bar. Pray for them, talk to them but choose the right association. They don't necessarily need to be your friends but souls that must be won for Christ.

Walk in the wisdom of God as you live before the unbelievers, and make it your duty to make him known.

Col 4: 5 (TPT)

Our association matters, it is important we walk with people who help us grow not only spiritually but also in all areas. Walk with people who have vision, women who are ready to challenge the status quo. As children of light and daughters of Zion we are told in the scriptures to choose our company carefully.

Don't continue to team up with believers in mismatched alliances, for what partnership is there righteousness and rebellion? Who could mingle light and darkness? What harmony can there be between Christ and Satan? Or what does a believer have in common with an unbeliever? What friendship does God's temple have with demons? For indeed, we are the temple of the living God, just as God has said: I will make my home in them and walk among them. I will be their God, and they will be my people. For this reason, come out from among them and be separate, says the Lord. 'Touch nothing that is unclean, and I will embrace you. I will be a true father to you, and you will be my beloved sons and daughters', says the Lord Yahweh Almighty.

2 Corinthians 6: 14 – 18 (TPT)

Thankfulness

On your feet now – applaud God! Bring a gift of laughter, sing yourselves into his presence. Know this; God is God, and God, God. He made us; we didn't make him. We are his people, his well – tended sheep. Enter with password. 'Thank you!' make yourselves at home, talking

praise. Thank him. Worship him. For God is sheer beauty, all generous in love, loyal always and ever.

Psalm 100: 1 – 5 (MSG)

Always say 'Thank you Jesus!' every time when everything is working, when things are not working, when you wake up in the morning, when you are about to sleep, when it looks like you can't find God around you. Thank him for that is the will of God and God inhabits the praises of his people.

Although the fig tree shall not blossom, neither shall fruit be in the vines; the labour of the olive shall fail, and the fields shall yield no meat; the flock shall be cut off from the fold, and there shall be no herd in the stall. Yet I will rejoice in the Lord, I will joy in the God of my salvation. The Lord is my strength, and he will make my feet like hinds' feet, and he will make me to walk upon mine high places.

Habakkuk 3: 17 – 19 (KJV)

When it looks like things are not going your way or you cannot feel the love of God. Are you weary or heavy laden? Habakkuk went through a tough time as well when it looked like everything was failing and his world was slowly crumbling. Giving God thanks at this point is one of the most difficult things to do because it takes a joyful heart to give thanks. Habakkuk chose to be confident in God and said "Yet" he will rejoice in the Lord because he knew so well that many are the afflictions of the righteous but the Lord delivered him out of them all.

So wake up, you living gateways! Lift up your heads, you ageless doors of destiny! Welcome the king of Glory, for he is about to come through you. You ask, "Who is this Glory- king?" the Lord, armed and ready for battle, the mighty one, invincible in every way! So wake up, you living gateways, and rejoice! Fling wide, you ageless doors of destiny! Here he comes; the King of Glory is ready to come in. You ask, "Who is this King of Glory?" He is the Lord of victory, armed and ready for battle, the mighty one, and invincible commander of heaven's hosts! Yes, he is the King of Glory.

Psalm 24: 7 – 10 (TPT)

At the sound of praise, gates are lifted up. The everlasting mountains are scattered, and the perpetual hills bow. Psalm 114 says "the sea saw them, and fled: Jordan was driven back. The mountains skipped like rams, and little hills like lambs." When we praise God our problems tremble at the presence of God and draw backward while we move forward.

It gets easier for us to thank God when we draw our mind back to the good things He has done for us and our family. Our thoughts matter in how much we thank him.

So keep your thoughts continually fixed on all that is authentic and real, honourable and admirable, beautiful and respectful, pure and holy, merciful and kind. And fasten your thoughts on every glorious work of God, praising him always.

Phil 4:8 (TPT)

CHAPTER 5

WE ARE IN THE DAYS OF REVIVAL!

A revival is the move of God among his people to move them forward, making them change agents and solution providers to their generation. A revival makes you a woman of impact.

Fear not o land; be glad and rejoice! For the Lord will do great things. Be not afraid, ye beasts of the field: for the pastures of the wilderness do spring, for the tree beareth her fruit, the fig tree and the field do yield their strength. Be glad then, ye children of Zion, and rejoice in the Lord your God: for he hath given us the former rain moderately, and he will cause to come down for you the rain, the former rain, and the latter rain in the first month. And the floors shall be full of wheat, and the fats shall overflow with wine and oil. And I will restore to you the years that the locust hath eaten, the cankerworm, and the caterpillar, and the palmerworm, and my great army which I sent among you. And ye shall eat in plenty and be satisfied, and praise the name of the Lord your God that hath dealt wondrously with you and my people shall never be ashamed. And it shall come to pass afterwards, that I will pour out my spirit upon all flesh; and your sons and daughters shall prophesy, your old men shall dream dreams, your young men shall see visions. And upon the servants and upon the handmaids in those days will I pour out my spirit.

Joel 2: 21 – 29 (KJV)

We are in the days of revival when God will pour out his spirit upon all flesh. There will be a great outpouring in the last days and we are in the last days. We have started seeing the strange and strong move of God upon the nations of the earth and many more people are now filled with passion for the things of God's kingdom. Women who will be used by God for these strange acts will yet arise like they arose in the bible and in history.

The spirit of the Lord is upon me; because the Lord hath anointed me to preach good tidings unto the meek; he hath sent me to bind up the brokenhearted, to proclaim liberty to the captives, and the opening of prison to them that are bound. To proclaim the acceptable year of the

Lord, and the day of vengeance of our God; to comfort all that mourn; to appoint unto them that mourn in Zion, to give them beauty for ashes, the oil of joy for mourning, the garment of praise for the spirit of heaviness, that they might be called the trees of righteousness, the planting of the Lord, that he might be glorified.

Isaiah 61: 1 – 3 (KJV)

That is what the spirit of the Lord does in a revival. When the spirit of the Lord comes upon a woman in a revival, she becomes a tool in the hands of God. We are in the Last days where the army of the Lord will arise. Many will begin to seek the face of God more than ever and we will be among this great move of God and become a part of this army.

And the inhabitants of one city shall go to another, saying, let us go speedily to pray before the Lord, and to seek the Lord of hosts: I will go also. Yea, many people and strong nations shall come to seek the Lord of hosts in Jerusalem, and to pray before the Lord.

Thus saith the Lord of hosts; in those days it shall come to pass, that ten men shall take hold out of all languages of the nations, even shall take hold of the skirt of him that is a Jew, saying, we will go with you: for we have heard that God is with you.

Zechariah 8: 21 – 23 (KJV)

In those days an army of the Lord will arise:

- An army of intercessors.
- An army of worshippers.
- An army of women who will put smiles on the faces of people out there with their genuine love for humanity and with their giving.
- An army of women that will take the good news of Jesus to the world.
- Women who will put their hands on the plough and not look back. They are ready to live for Jesus regardless of the cost.

A fire devoureth before them; and behind them a flame burneth! The land is as the garden of Eden before them, and behind them a desolate wilderness; yea, and nothing shall escape them. The appearance of them

is as the appearance of horses; and as horsemen, so shall they run. Like the noise of chariots on the top of mountains shall they leap, like the noise of a flame of fire that devoureth the stubble, as a strong people set in a battle array. Before their faces the people shall be much pained: all faces shall gather blackness. They shall run like mighty men; they shall climb the wall like men of war; and they shall march every one of his ways, and they shall not break their ranks. Neither shall one thrust another; they shall walk everyone in his path: and when they fall upon the sword they shall not be wounded.

Joel 2: 3 – 8 (KJV)

This is an army of people to be feared. They are caught up in a revival, nothing can hurt them, they run like mighty men, they walk everyone in his path means they walk in their God – given assignment. They know their purpose on earth and they walk in it. They know the 'I am that I am lives in them'. They know they have God's presence in their lives. They know they will scale strange, unimaginable heights because they are caught up in a revival.

God is saying to his precious daughter:

Awake, awake; put on thy strength O Zion. Shake thyself from the dust, arise. How beautiful upon the mountains are the feet of him that bringeth good tidings, that publisheth peace; that bringeth good tidings of good that publisheth salvation; that saith unto Zion, thy God reigneth!

Isaiah 52: 1,2,7

Awake, o, sleeper, and arise.

Eph 5:14

How do we know we are in a revival?

We are in a revival when we want more of God; when we want to see other people saved; when Matthew 6: 33 becomes our watch word; when our heart begins to pant after God.; when we begin to do the things of God with delight and we don't see intercession for lost souls as a burden;

when our heart aches to see lost souls or even people in the church who have not experienced a revival yet.

How do we get here?

1. We must cry out to God to revive us. Psalm 42:1

It takes a sincere cry to God to get here because we cannot do it in the energy of the flesh for the spirit is willing but the flesh is weak. It is the Holy spirit that empowers us for effective walk with God. When the spirit of God comes upon us, our walk for God becomes more exciting and not burdensome. I went to God many times praying for this so you can go to God and tell him you need grace. Many at times we want to serve God, there are a lot of things we want to do to make God pleased with us. We see women or people on fire for God and we wonder when we will ever get to that stage. I was once like that, I condemned myself for not growing spiritually. I saw a lot of people especially women doing great things for God and disliked myself the more for not being able to do what they are doing for God. I never went to God for help during those times because I felt God was disappointed in me and condemned me and I tried several times in my own power and failed, so God is the one who can help you serve him effectively. Go to him asking him for grace he will help you because he said if you search for him with all your heart, you will find him (Jer 29: 13) and remember, "Blessed are they who hunger and thirst for righteousness for they shall be filled". Zech 4: 6 says "Not by power not by might but by my spirit saith the lord of host". Without the holy spirit, the Christian race becomes a burden. When you are in a revival, service to God becomes exciting, you feel this unexplainable joy you can't describe it. Without the Holy spirit Christianity has no beauty. The Holy spirit will help you pray, if you are struggling with prayer. I was there before I would sleep off when I wake up to pray. When you wake up to pray, worship God and pray in the Holy ghost then you get divine strength.

2. We must be ready to sacrifice our time, energy and pleasures of the world. Sometimes those pleasures may not mean sinful pleasures but excess comfort. Most times we will have to go out of our comfort zone to serve God.

3. Righteousness

Turn you at my reproof: behold, I will pour out my spirit unto you, I will make known my words unto you.

Prov 1: 23 (KJV)

It is impossible to encounter the rain of the spirit without righteousness. To experience this outpouring, there is a need to thirst for the rain of righteousness and fully surrender our lives to Jesus. Living in righteousness and letting go of every sin. We must work out our salvation.

You are passionate for righteousness and you hate lawlessness. This is why God, your God, crowns you with bliss above your fellow kings. He has anointed you, more than any other, with his oil of fervent joy, the very fragrance of heaven's gladness.

Psalm 45:7 (TPT)

Bishop David Oyedepo, in his book 'Manifestations of The Spirit' said: Everyone has a measure of unction, but your level of consecration is what determines the level of unction that God makes available to you. It is time we live in a genuine, unashamed righteousness.

The entire universe is standing on tip toe, yearning to see the unveiling of God's glorious sons and daughters.

Romans 8: 19 (TPT)

They are yearning to see your manifestation, waiting eagerly to see you emerge they are eager to see what will happen through you. Because there is a lot embedded in you. God has instilled so much in you. Because eyes have not seen, hears has not heard neither has it entered into the hearts of men what God has prepared for you (His lover).

Your lives light up the world. Let others see your light from a distance, for how can you hide a city that stands on a hilltop? And who would light a lamp and then hide it in an obscure place? Instead, it's placed where everyone in the house can benefit from its light. So don't hide your light! Let it shine brightly before others, so that the commendable things you do

will shine as light upon them, and then they will give their praise to your father in heaven.

Matthew 5: 14 – 16 (TPT)

The bible says you are the light of the world and a light stands out. In obscurity your light will shine for men to see. In verse 13 the scripture says you are the salt of the earth and the essence of salt is to sweeten and preserve from decadence so you are a salt ordained by God to sweeten people's lives and people around us should be glad they came across us because we lighten up and sweeten their lives.

The days of revival are the days of outpouring of the spirit of God upon all flesh and everyone who desires it will experience this outpouring.

The Holy Spirit will come upon us afresh in a mighty way, the kind we have never seen before. The things they saw and did in the early days were amazing but the things we will see in these last days; the acts of God through us will be mind blowing. As the Holy Spirit comes upon us heavily, we begin to exercise authority. Luke 10: 19 says "I have given you authority over principalities and powers and over all the powers of the enemy and nothing shall by any means hurt you." And we are made to understand from the scriptures that Christ translated us from the kingdom of darkness to light. At the point of redemption authority was conferred on us to walk in dominion over the powers of darkness. Whether you know it or not, the moment you gave your life to Christ you received dominion, how much more when the Holy Spirit comes upon us in fullness. Oh! Spirit of the Living God we are thirsty for you. We can do strange acts; command signs and wonders through the help of the Holy Spirit and in the name of Jesus.

Prayer:

Spirit of the Living God, I release myself to you today for an outpouring of your spirit upon me. For it is written that you Lord will pour out your spirit upon all flesh. Holy spirit I receive an outpouring today. Breathe upon me because I cannot do it without you, I can't

experience a revival without you. So dear Lord Jesus I receive a fresh baptism of the revival fire of the holy ghost upon me right now, let it burn within me and let me be part of the end – time revivalists. Let my light so shine for all to see. Let me become a woman of impact indeed let me become a global phenomenon that great things will happen through me and let me become a woman after God's own heart. I pray this in Faith and in the name of Jesus amen.

Let's declare this (It's a prayer declaration) put your name there:

Awake, awake ---------- as a change agent. Just like Deborah arose awake. The world awaits your manifestation. Awake! To fulfill God's plan for your life Awake! So that your name will be heard in high places, for you are a light to the world a city set upon a hill that cannot be hidden. Awake! Oh ---------- for God has ordained you a fame and a praise. Awake! So you can be part of this strong move of God. Awake! God created you for a purpose and refuse to settle for less. I will make marks and impacts that my generations yet unborn will enjoy from.

The scripture says:

The harvest is huge and ripe. But there are not enough harvesters to bring it all in.

Luke 10:2

Blessedness of a revival

Arise, shine; for thy light is come, and the glory of the Lord is upon thee. For, behold, the darkness shall cover the earth, and gross darkness the people: but the Lord shall arise upon thee, and his glory shall be seen upon thee. And the Gentiles shall come to thy light, and kings to the brightness of thy rising.

Isaiah 60: 1 – 3 (KJV)

A revival time is a season of glory!

But in the last days it shall come to pass, that the mountain of the house of the Lord shall be established in the top of the mountains, and it shall be exalted above the hills; and people shall flow into it. And many nations shall come, and say, come, let us go up to the mountain of the Lord, and to the house of the God of Jacob; and he will teach us his ways, and we will walk in his paths: for the law shall go forth from Zion, and the word of the Lord from Jerusalem. And he shall judge among many people, and rebuke strong nations afar off; and they shall beat their swords into plow shares, and their spears into pruning hooks: nation shall not lift up a sword against nation; neither shall they learn war any more. But they shall sit every man under his vine and under his fig tree; and none shall make them afraid: for the mouth of the Lord of hosts hath spoken it. For all people will walk everyone in the name of his god, and we will walk in the name of the Lord our God forever and ever. In that day, saith the Lord, will I assemble her that halteth, and I will gather her that is driven out, and her that I have afflicted. And I will make her that halteth a remnant, and I will gather her that is driven out, and her that I have afflicted.

Micah 4: 1 – 7 (KJV)

Sing, o daughter of Zion; shout, o Israel; be glad and rejoice with all the heart, o daughter of Jerusalem. The Lord hath taken away thy judgements, he hath cast out thine enemy: the king of Israel, even the Lord, is in the midst of thee: thou shalt not see evil anymore. In that day it shall be said to Jerusalem, fear thou not: and to Zion, let not thine hands be slack. The Lord thy God in the midst of thee is mighty; he will save, he will rejoice over thee with Joy; he will rest in his love, he will joy over thee with singing. I will gather them that are sorrowful for the solemn assembly, who are of thee, to whom the reproach of it was burden. Behold, at that time I will undo all that afflict thee: and I will save her that halteth, and gather her that was driven out; and I will get them praise and fame in every land where they have been put to shame. At that time will I bring you again, even in the time that I gather you: for I will make you a name and a praise among all people of the earth, when I turn back your captivity before your eyes, saith the Lord.

Zephaniah 3: 14 – 20 (KJV)

In the last days, the days of Revival! God comes to dwell with his people. Psalm 46: 5 says God is in the midst of her, she shall not be moved. In the Last days we enjoy divine presence and God changes the stories of his people. He gives us a name of distinction; he restores to us all that we have lost in the time of ignorance to the devil. God beautifies and honors his people in a revival. A Revival time is a Season of Glory!

We must keep the fire of revival ever burning.

The fire must be kept burning on the altar continuously; it must not go out.

Leviticus 6: 13 (NIV)

The fire shall keep burning on our prayer altars and the love of God shall keep burning in our hearts in Jesus name amen.

Conclusion:

So until I come, be diligent in devouring the word of God, be faithful in prayer, and in teaching the believers.

1 Tim 4: 13 (TPT)

But you, my delightfully loved friends, constantly and progressively build yourselves up on the foundation of your most holy faith by praying every moment in the spirit.

Jude 1: 20 (TPT)

Let us continually build ourselves up in faith doing the will of God. Jesus is sitting at the right side of the father advocating for us.

God will continually revitalize you, implanting within you the passion to do what pleases him.

Phil 2: 13 (TPT)

The Holy Spirit of God has sealed you in Jesus Christ until you experience your full salvation. So never grieve the Spirit of God or take for granted his holy influence in your life.

Ephesians 4: 30 (TPT)

And finally; God's beloved daughter;

Until we all experience the fullness of what it means to know the son of God, and finally we become one perfect man with the full dimensions of spiritual maturity and fully developed in the abundance of Christ.

Eph 4: 13 (TPT)

THE WOMAN GOD USES IS THE WOMAN IN A REVIVAL! AND THE WOMAN IN A REVIVAL IS THE WOMAN FULLY YIELDED TO GOD!

SALUTE TO YOU WOMAN AFTER GOD'S OWN HEART, 'A CHANGE AGENT'.

PEACE TO YOU, IN JESUS NAME. AMEN.

PERSONAL AND BOLD DECLARATIONS OF FAITH:

- For whatsoever is born of God overcometh the world. I am born of God; therefore, I am an overcomer.1 john 5:4
- Because he that cometh from above is above all; therefore, I am above life situations and circumstances. I am above failure. I am above sickness and diseases. I am above shame and reproach. John 3:31
- Because Jesus lives in me, I have nothing to fear. For greater is he that is in me than he that is in the world. 1 john 4:4, 1 peter 3: 13
- I am a change agent and an end time savior. Obadiah 1:21
- I am a lover of God and a woman after God's own heart.
- My father, the I am that I am, has instilled greatness inside of me, things that eyes have not seen, they have not heard of it before, nobody has imagined it before, it has never crossed the hearts of men, greatness that will make people open their mouths wide in wonder has been embedded in me from creation and I will manifest it. Jer 1: 5
- I am a god and the daughter of the Most High. Psalm 82:6
- I am heavily guarded and surrounded by heavenly immunities; I enjoy the presence of God for I am joined in life-union with Jesus.
- I am part of the army of God. I am Revival!
- I am filled with the power of God to do signs and wonders. Micah 3: 8
- Kings shall come to my rising for I am favoured and blessed and in all I do I shall prosper. Isaiah 60: 2
- I am a royal diadem in the hands of the Father. Isaiah 62: 3
- I am called Hephzibah because God delights in me. Isaiah 62: 4

CLOSING NOTE FROM THE AUTHOR (I to the amazing people who read this book)

Philippians 3: 12 – 14 (TPT)

I admit that I haven't yet acquired the absolute fullness that I'm pursuing, but I run with passion into his abundance so that I may reach the purpose that Jesus Christ wants me to fulfill and discover. I don't depend on my own strength to accomplish this; however, I do have compelling focus: I forget all of the past as I fasten my heart to the future instead. I run straight for the divine invitation of reaching the heavenly goal and gaining the victory prize through the anointing of Jesus.

The books below are journals that can help with Bible study, serve as church notebook and as prayer journal. Inside of these books are personal declarations to bless your day. They are available on Amazon.

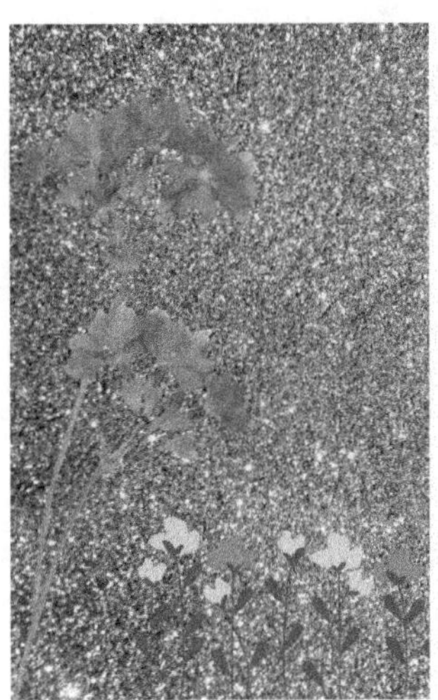

ABOUT THE AUTHOR

The author of this book, Favour A.O, is a growing believer who is passionate about seeing believers especially women, gain confidence in Christ; fulfill purpose and enjoy God's love through building an intimate relationship with God. This is her first book.

Forward your questions, experiences while reading and prayers to favour.a.mjk.26@gmail,com

www.ingramcontent.com/pod-product-compliance
Lightning Source LLC
LaVergne TN
LVHW010500160826
845677LV00012B/2582

* 9 7 9 8 3 5 1 1 4 6 2 2 5 *